Using Coupons Strategically To Save BIG

S. Denise Hoyle

DEDICATION

This book is dedicated to frugal shoppers and everyone who must live within a budget. We will help you save on the things you need so you can spend on the things you want!.

CONTENTS

1 Locate Resources for Obtaining Coupons

The best place to find coupons is in your Sunday newspaper. If you don't already subscribe to the paper, you may be able to choose to have only the Sunday newspaper delivered. Of course you could always go to the store each Sunday to buy a copy (or several), or you could get a discounted subscription by ordering online at DiscountedNewspapers.com or Subscription-Offers.com.

Once you've got the hang of strategic couponing you'll probably want to buy several copies of the newspaper each week. Be sure to check the 2014 Schedule of Coupon Inserts below so that you'll know ahead of time if there will be coupon inserts in the paper and how many to expect. Most weeks there will be at least two coupon inserts, one each from Red Plum and Smart Source. Occasionally you will also find a Proctor & Gamble insert as well. Don't forget to look for coupons in the store inserts such as CVS, RiteAid, Target, Walgreens, and your local grocery store.

The Internet is also a wonderful place to get coupons. Many manufacturer and retailer websites will post coupons for their products, as will some drug stores and super centers, but you'll find the majority of printable online coupons at Coupons.com and the websites of the companies that print the weekly newspaper inserts (i.e. RedPlum.com, SmartSource.com). There are also a few new services that allow users to download coupons to their cell phone or rewards card. These coupons are typically deducted at checkout when you present your rewards card, or in the case of UPromise, the money is added to a college fund that you setup as you wish. Following is a list of all the top coupon sites.

Printable Coupons

- BettyCrocker – http://www.bettycrocker.com/coupons
- Coupon Bug – http://www.couponbug.com
- Coupons.com – http://www.coupons.com
- Eat Better America – http://www.eatbetteramerica.com/coupons/

- Penny Pincher Gazette –
  http://www.ppgazette.com
- Redplum – http://redplum.com
- Ready, Set, Eat –
  http://www.readyseteat.com/
- SmartSource – http://smartsource.com
- Whole Foods Market –
  http://wholefoodsmarket.com/coupons/

Downloadable Coupons

- Cellfire.com
- UPromise.com
- CouponSherpa.com

2 Determine Which Coupons to Cut

I've always clipped coupons, but before I became a strategic couponer I only clipped the coupons for products that I already used and threw the rest away. My theory was that if I bought a product I didn't normally use just because I had a coupon, then I wasn't really saving any money. I have since learned that through strategic couponing I can get many products for free, or close to free, if I'm willing to try out new brands. In fact, one of the best things about strategic couponing for me is that my family of seven is now able to try any number of name brand products, and we don't have to settle for generics or the cheapest products on the market any more.

To take best advantage of available deals, I highly recommend that you clip EVERY coupon you find, no matter if it's for a product you may use or not. Keep two separate stashes of coupons – the ones you may possibly use, and the ones that you're pretty sure you won't use. For example, I clip every coupon I find – from magazines, newspapers, inserts – and I organize all the ones I could potentially use in my Coupon clutch binder (http://couponclutch.com), and I keep all the rest in a small check file for potential trades. Although I don't need denture adhesive, I will keep coupons for it to trade with someone who does. It is illegal to buy or sell coupons, however it is perfectly fine to trade coupons so there are several active forums for trading coupons like A Full Cup (http://afullcup.com) and Hot Coupon World (http://hotcouponworld.com).

There are a couple of options if you're buying multiple newspapers for the inserts. Some people like to get multiple coupon inserts and clip them all. Some people like to get multiple coupon inserts but only clip and file one set, while keeping the extra copies in file folders organized by date. And then there are people like me who get one subscription but buy multiple papers on "good coupon" weeks, and I file them all by date. I only clip these coupons when I'm ready to use them. You can search the coupon databases at A Full Cup or Hot Coupon World and quickly locate the file for the appropriate coupon and clip as needed, saving the time of clipping and filing every coupon. Another idea for those buy a large volume of inserts is to buy the newspaper in multiples of two (so 2, 4 or 6 papers depending on the coupons available) then tear each insert into individual pages and stack the matching pages. If you only have two papers then just stack them and cut two pages at a time. If you have four or more papers then take the stacks and staple them together on one side, making sure not to staple through any coupons, which helps to keep the pages stable while you cut through them all at once.

You can start slowly if you'd like, or try out a few different methods to see what works best for you. The beauty of strategic couponing is that you can decide how much or how little time you want to spend, and if you keep your coupon stash well organized then you will save yourself a LOT of time AND money!

3 Organize Your Coupons

A great way to organize your coupons is to use baseball card style plastic organizer pages in a three ring binder. You can even get a pretty one that you won't mind carrying around with you from CouponClutch.com. Mine came with a Deluxe Coupon Organizer System that includes 8 tabbed dividers, 3 full page plastic binder pages, 10 nine pocket pages, 10 eight pocket pages, 10 six pocket pages and 10 three pocket pages. I keep the three full page plastic pages at the rear of the binder and use them for my three favorite stores. For example, I use mine for Publix, Walgreens and CVS. I keep the weekly sales flyer in the front of the plastic page and any rebates or additional store flyers (like the Publix green advantage) on the backside of the pocket. I keep a 3-pocket coupon page behind each store pocket and I keep store coupons in the top pocket, rainchecks in the bottom pocket, and the coupons

I'm planning to use at that store during the current week in the middle pocket.

The tabbed dividers are meant to be placed in the front of the binder with one each of the 9-pocket pages, 8-pocket pages and 6-pocket pages behind each tab. Most of your coupons will fit in the 9-pocket pages so those should go first. When placing your Internet printables or similarly sized coupons sideways in the pockets, be sure to position them with the product picture at the top so that you only need to flip through them without removing them from the pocket to find the coupons you need. Odd shaped or oversized coupons can be placed in the 6-pocket and 3-pocket pages. Any extra coupon pages can be placed behind the tabbed divider categories that you use most. I keep mine in alphabetical order in the pockets, but you'll figure out the method that works best for you.

4 Learn How to Maximize Your Savings

The magic of strategic couponing happens when you ONLY buy things that are on sale, and of course the few staples (milk, eggs, etc) that you need for the week. The trick here is to stockpile items when they're on sale so that you're always paying the lowest possible price for the things you need and use. Instead of buying enough coffee for the week, you get enough for the month while it's on sale, and instead of buying enough toothpaste or toilet paper for the month, you buy enough for six months when you can get it on sale. It won't take long, and once you've built up a bit of a stockpile you'll see how easy it can be to get those high numbers like 70-90% off.

There are so many wonderful resources online that you can find out everything you need to know for free, but if you'd prefer to learn one on one from a teacher or through a workshop, there are plenty of those available as well. Take advantage of websites like ShopperStrategy.com and subscribe to or follow money saving blogs based in your local area to maximize your savings. Don't limit yourself to your local area, also look for sites that focus on your favorite stores or blogs that follow national chains and you'll get all kinds of free information sent directly to your inbox or RSS reader.

The stores I visit most often are Publix, CVS and Walgreens so I follow several bloggers that do matchups of coupons and sales for those stores like I Heart Publix, Wild For Wags and Simply CVS. Every week when planning my shopping trip(s) I copy the matchups for each store and paste them into a Word document that I name based on the store and the date I plan to shop there (i.e. publix_101814.docx, cvs_093014). I sit in front of the computer with my coupon clutch and go through the list one item at a time. I delete the items from the list that I'm not interested in and pull or print all the matching coupons before I print the final list that I'll carry to the store with me. I put all of the coupons that I plan to use in the side pocket inside my coupon clutch, then carry the whole thing into the store with me so I have the others handy in case I find any in store deals or clearance items that I can further discount with a coupon.

Remember, strategic couponing is a learning experience and it will take a little time to get the hang of it, but it really is fun and the more you save the more you'll enjoy it! On my first few attempts at strategic couponing I only saved about 40-50%, but I was THRILLED with that since it can get pretty expensive to feed a large family like mine, or really any family for that matter. Now I routinely save between 70-90% and I keep track of my savings because I love to see how I'm doing and to share the deal information with others who might be interested (i.e. brag to my mom and friends).

5 Maintain Your Coupon Stash

As you're going through your coupons to plan your shopping trips each week you should be on the lookout for an6y expired or soon to be expired coupons. Remove the expired ones and keep an eye out for any valuable soon-to-be expired coupons that you may not want to miss out on using. Also be sure to keep any duplicates together in your binder so you can easily tell how many you have of each specific coupon.

If you've found a particularly interesting deal and you don't have enough coupons then search for some more to add to your stash by searching for coupons at eBay, pay a clipping service like Select Coupon or head back to A Full Cup or Hot Coupon World and trade for the coupons you need.

2014 Coupon Insert Schedule

January
5 — (2) Redplum, (2) Smart Source
12 — Redplum & Smart Source
19 — Smart Source
26 — (2) Redplum & Smart Source & Procter and Gamble

February
2 — Redplum & Smart Source
9 — Redplum & Smart Source
16 — Redplum
23 — Smart Source

March
2 — Redplum & Smart Source & Procter and Gamble
9 — Redplum & Smart Source
16 — Redplum & Smart Source
23 — Redplum & Smart Source
30 — Redplum & Smart Source & Procter and Gamble

April
6 — (2) Redplum & Smart Source
13 — Redplum & Smart Source
20 — **No Inserts (Easter)**
27 — Redplum & Smart Source & Procter and Gamble

May

4 — Redplum & Smart Source

11 — Redplum & Smart Source & Procter and Gamble

18 — Redplum & (2) Smart Source

25 — **No Inserts (Memorial Day)**

June

1 — Redplum & Smart Source & Procter and Gamble

8 — Smart Source

15 — Redplum & Smart Source

22 — Redplum & Smart Source

29 — Redplum & Smart Source

July

6 — Procter and Gamble

13 — Redplum & Smart Source & Purina

20 — **No Inserts**

27 — (2) Redplum & (2) Smart Source & Procter and Gamble

August

3 — (2) Redplum & Smart Source

10 — Redplum & Smart Source

17 — Redplum & Smart Source

24 — Redplum & Smart Source

31 — Procter & Gamble

September

7 — Redplum & (2) Smart Source

14 — Redplum & Smart Source

21 — Smart Source

28 — Redplum & Smart Source & Procter and

Gamble

October
5 — Redplum & (2) Smart Source
12 — Redplum & Smart Source
19 — Smart Source & Little Tikes
26 — Redplum & Smart Source & Procter and Gamble

November
2 — Redplum & (2) Smart Source
9 — Redplum & Smart Source
16 — Redplum & Smart Source
23 — Redplum & Smart Source
30 — Procter & Gamble

December
7 — Redplum & (2) Smart Source
14 — Redplum & Smart Source
21 — No Inserts
28 — Procter and Gamble

Remember there is no schedule available for General Mills (GM) and Proctor & Gamble (P&G) inserts, so they may show up at any time!

ABOUT THE AUTHOR

Denise Hoyle is a professional blogger and Chief Frugal Officer of a family of six, including nine year old quadruplets and a ten year old. Denise is a frugal shop-a-holic with expensive tastes who likes the finer things but refuses to pay full price!